SANTA CLAUS AND HIS WORKS.

From houses and furniture, dishes and pans,
To bracelets and brooches, and bright colored fans,
And soldiers and pop-guns, and trumpets and drums,
To baby's tin rattle, and bright top which hums.

ALL FROM SANTA'S WORKSHOP.

And oh, the gay dollies with long curling hair,
That can open their eyes and sit up in a chair.
There old Santa will sit with his specs on his nose
And work all the day making pretty new clothes;

Such as dresses and sashes, and hats for the head,
And night-gowns to wear when they jump into bed;
And garters and socks, and the tiniest shoes,
And lots of nice things such as doll-babies use.

SANTA CLAUS AND HIS WORKS.

Then he makes with his tools many wonderful things,
Such as monkeys, and acrobats jumping on strings,
With many things more, for I can not tell half—
But just look at his picture, I'm sure you will laugh.

And a very wise fellow is Santa Claus, too,
He is jolly and kind, but he knows what to do;
And after his work for the day is all done,
As he sees the long rays of the bright setting sun,

He climbs to his turret, way up near the sky,
And looks o'er the world with his keen searching eye;
Peeps into the cities, the towns, great and small,
And villages too, for he's sure to see all.

He looks in the homes of the rich and the poor,
Of those who have plenty, and those who endure;
For God's little children he finds everywhere,
The rich and the poor are alike in his care.

FOR A YOUNG ARTIST.

SANTA CLAUS AND HIS WORKS.

FOR A GOOD GIRL.

How funny he looks as he stands to inspect
The tree that with gifts he has lavishly decked:
He is large round the waist, but what care we for that—
'Tis the good-natured people who always are fat.

I told you his home was up North by the Pole,
In a palace of ice, lives this happy old soul;
And the walls are as bright as the diamonds that shone
In the cave, where Aladdin went in, all alone,

To look for the lamp, which, we've often been told,
Turned iron and lead into silver and gold,
His bedstead is made of the ivory white,
And he sleeps on a mattress of down every night.

QUITE A SURPRISE!

SANTA CLAUS AND HIS WORKS.

For all the day long, he is working his best,
And surely at night, the old fellow should rest.
He uses no candle, for all through the night,
The Polar-star shining, looks in with its light.

Should he need for his breakfast a fish or some veal,
The sea-calves are his, and the whale, and the seal.
Where he lives there is always a cool pleasant air,
Last summer, oh! didn't we wish we were there?

He's a funny old chap, and quite shy, it would seem,
For I never but once caught a glimpse of his team;
'Twas a bright moonlight night, and it stood in full view,
So seeing it, I can describe it to you.

FOR A SPECIAL FAVORITE.

SANTA CLAUS AND HIS WORKS.

When Christmas time comes, he will toil like a Turk,
For the cheery old fellow is happy at work.
With his queer-looking team, through the air he will go
And alight on the houses, all white with the snow;

And into the chimneys will dart in a trice,
When all are asleep, but the cat and the mice;
And he has to be quick, to be through in a night,
For his work must be done ere the coming of light.

Then he'll fill up the stockings with candy and toys,
And all without making a bit of a noise,
There'll be presents for Julia, and Bettie, and Jack,
And plenty more left in the old fellow's sack.

And if Evrie behaves well, and minds what is said,
Quits teasing the cat, and goes early to bed,
He'll find for his present a sled, or a gun,
A ready companion in frolic and fun.

SANTA CLAUS AND HIS WORKS.

His house in fair Santa Claus-ville, as you know,
Is near the North Pole, in the ice and the snow;
But clothed all in fur from his head to his toes,
Not a feeling of sadness the old fellow knows.

He has the most beautiful long snowy hair,

Though the top of his head is quite shiny and bare;
His dear little eyes how they twinkle and shine,
But he never was known to drink brandy or wine.

'Tis only because he is merry and bright
That they sparkle like two little stars of the night,
And perhaps 'tis his kindness of heart showing through,
While he's planning and working dear children for you.

For good little children he's working away,
Making the toys which he'll bring them some day;
And busy all day, while he whistles and sings,
He's planning and making the funniest things.